ALAN KNOTT ON
WICKET-KEEPING

ALAN KNOTT ON
WICKET-KEEPING

Stanley Paul, London

Stanley Paul & Co Ltd
3 Fitzroy Square, London W1P 6JD

An Imprint of the Hutchinson Publishing Group

London Melbourne Sydney Auckland
Wellington Johannesburg and agencies
throughout the world

First published 1977
© Alan Knott 1977
Drawings © Stanley Paul & Co Ltd 1977

Set in Monotype Gill Sans Light

Printed in Great Britain by litho at
The Anchor Press Ltd and bound by
Wm Brendon & Son Ltd, both of
Tiptree, Essex

ISBN 0 09 129470 3 (cased)
0 09 129471 1 (paper)

Acknowledgements

The author and publishers would like to thank
Patrick Eagar for the many excellent photographs
which he took specially for this book.

Other copyright photographs are acknowledged
as follows: Central Press 3, 56; Sports and
General 4, 55; Yorkshire Evening Post 45.

Contents

Preface

As far back as I can remember, the life of a professional sportsman has always seemed very exciting. I was very lucky to become a cricketer and I know there are many other young lads who feel like me, drawn to the game as if to a magnet.

In this book I hope you will find the guidance you need to progress and to enjoy the game more at your own particular level.

Equally, I hope you can learn from my experiences and ideas and that you will never fall into the trap of thinking that you know it all. Remember there is always more to learn. As a boy I can recall being greedy to learn and I still feel that way now.

Cricket has so many fascinating points as well as the very important ones of gathering runs and bowling out the opposition. There's the approach to the game, understanding the different tactics and strategies involved, learning to handle pressure, and the many other aspects of the game which make it so absorbing.

Dedication is of course an essential attribute for any young cricketer who wishes to become a professional. Even if he reaches Test status his earnings won't compare with those of the soccer, golf and tennis stars. So your chief reason for making cricket a career will simply be that it is the thing you want to do most of all.

You will be working at your chosen game seven days a week, something which is often forgotten by many people who say they envy my life. But I never forget that I am involved in my chosen profession, doing something I want to do.

A cricketer can express himself through his talent and can give much pleasure to others.

It's not an easy life – indeed it's a most taxing one – but I've found cricket a career that's given me tremendous pleasure and made it possible for me to travel not only all over the country but all over the world.

Yes, I've enjoyed playing cricket – I hope this book will help you to enjoy the game too.

1. Got it at last – my 220th Test victim – Lawrence Rowe, stumped off the bowling of Derek Underwood in the Fifth Test against the West Indies at the Oval in 1976. This dismissal enabled me to break the world wicket-keeping Test record held by Godfrey Evans.

2. As Lawrence Rowe begins the walk back to the pavilion the congratulations start.

Introduction to wicket-keeping

To be a wicket-keeper is one of the most demanding of jobs in any sport. It needs stamina, alertness, concentration and, of course, ability.

A wicket-keeper can be bobbing up and down for five hours out of six, sometimes for two days running, and possibly into a third. He must stretch or dive to the wide ones, jump high when required and be ready for a sprint to the wicket when he is standing back. It is hard work, but a wonderfully rewarding job, because you are never out of the game. No greater thrill exists for me than to take off, stretching every inch of legs, body and arms, to claw a wide deflection into my eager gloves.

What are the main essentials of wicket-keeping? Really there are two – an ability to sight the ball early and then to catch it whether it comes from a delivery, a hit or a throw in.

Catching methods

Methods of catching vary slightly. Some 'keepers place their little fingers together, others cross the little finger of one hand over that of the other, and I, in fact, catch with my right crossed over my left.

3. Here at Perth in the Second Test (1970), Doug Walters' deflection off Peter Lever was slowed up by his pad and helped me to take this catch wide on the leg side.

4. Mushtaq Mohammad just gets home in time in the Second Test between England and Pakistan at Lord's, August 1974.

Older 'keepers will tell you how their hands become gnarled and twisted from bad knocks. Today, fortunately, gloves offer far more protection, with the fingers reinforced with rubber stalls.

One frequent cause of injury is in catching consistently with the fingers pointing at the ball. When impact comes right on the tips, there is tremendous resistance against the ball and a finger can be badly jarred or even broken. So catch with the fingers pointing down if the ball is below chest height. As your hands come to chest level, your fingers will naturally start to point at the ball (photo 5). In this situation, I always try to move my body either inside or outside the line of flight, and turn my shoulders to take the ball with my fingers pointing outwards (photo 6). If the ball comes above chest height, then the fingers should be pointing upwards (photo 7).

On taking the ball, you must 'give', if only slightly, with the hands continuing back on the same line (photos 8 and 9) so reducing the resistance and the risk of the ball jumping out of the gloves. This 'giving' also helps to prevent bruising. But avoid exaggerating or hurrying this movement which, if accentuated, could take your gloves off the line of the ball. Try not to keep the fingers rigid. They should form a relaxed cup, padded cushions into which the ball will sink and remain.

Co-ordination

Co-ordination of body and mind is essential for good wicket-keeping and one's reactions, no matter whether above average or not, can always

9

5

6

7

be sharpened still more by hard work and assiduous training. Once the ball is sighted, you want your body to react instantly to the message flashed from the brain as to the right way to take it.

The MCC *Cricket Coaching Book* includes a fine chapter on group work in which are described different exercises suited for every physical movement needed to play the game. Say, for example, you want to sharpen up on diving to those wide deflections. First, think out the movements that are necessary and then go through them physically in slow motion, preferably with a coach or friend watching. Ask him to lob a ball to either side of you so that you have to dive for it. As you improve, you can have the ball thrown under-arm quicker and quicker until it is coming at a realistic speed. Then, in a match, with the body trained to respond instantly to the brain's demands, you will find yourself flying to take the catch when the thick edge off the pace bowler comes along.

Frequently the assertion is made that wicket-keepers are born and not made. Yet anyone with average ball sense can make a fair job of it if he is prepared to work hard.

I am by nature a little stiff physically which

accounts for all my loosening and stretching exercises because it is absolutely vital to be as supple as you can be and stay that way.

Courage

'Keepers need courage, especially when they are learning the art. Standing up to the wicket can prompt the fear that the ball might be deflected off bat or stumps and strike you. Such dangers will become much more real if you blink, flinch or turn your head away as the batsman plays his shot. It is when you are not watching the ball that the risk of injury is greatest because you do not know where it is. So fight any such fears and never turn your head away, unless as a last resort when there is nothing else you can do to prevent the ball from hitting you in the face.

10. Diving again – the victim is Mankad in the 1974 Test against India at Edgbaston off the bowling of Geoff Arnold. This was a very wide deflection and it's the furthest I've ever dived to take a catch. I took the ball with my right hand in front of Keith Fletcher's right shin – he's at first slip.

8

9

10

11

Mind training and concentration

Mentally, you must build up your powers of concentration to a point where you believe every ball bowled will come to you. As the bowler approaches the wicket, think only of the fact that he is bowling at you. Never feel that the batsman is certain to hit the ball, even if it is only a slow full toss, and dismiss from your mind any thought that the ball is going to hit the wicket or the batsman's body.

As you move up through the grades of cricket, such concentration becomes more difficult, because pitches and batsmen are better, so that at Test level you reach a situation where the number of deliveries coming through to you is comparatively small. On the MCC under-25 tour of Pakistan, Derek Underwood bowled for nearly two hours without my taking a single delivery. Then suddenly one beat the bat. I caught it cleanly, but only because I had been taking all the previous deliveries in my mind.

With the mind trained in this way, there should also be a slightly aggressive attitude. You *want* the ball to come through and you *want* the batsman to give you a chance of dismissing him. After all, the aim is to put out the opposition as quickly as possible. This approach kindles the enthusiasm, the bounce and the energy needed to do the job to the full, and to go for every chance, however impossible it might seem.

Who will ever forget the almost unbelievable Godfrey Evans. Even when I saw him after he had retired from county cricket I could not fail to be impressed by his incredible bounce and his eagerness to be involved and go for everything.

Patience is a virtue

Patience is a further necessary virtue. Even though you may be itching to be in the action, to catch, stump or run out a batsman, you must be prepared to await your opportunity. Every day presents a physical and mental challenge. You must be just as prepared to take a chance off the last ball of the day as the first, and never surrender to the view that, because you have not touched the ball for some time, nothing is going to come your way. In county cricket, days pass without a chance, and then possibly two or three come in the space of a couple of overs.

Perfection

Perfection must be the target, checking all the time that mind and body are functioning properly. That is why I make a point of trying to catch every ball that comes my way, even when it is very wide of the stumps. It is much better to try to catch the ball cleanly rather than being satisfied with parrying it, since the 'keeper with the right habit has a far better chance of holding a deflection off the bat. Aiming for perfection promotes reliability and consistency. It cannot be good having a 'keeper who is brilliant one day and dreadful the next, or one who takes the hard catches and drops the easy ones. These faults usually arise through lack of concentration and patience.

Missed chances

A missed chance must not be allowed to affect your performance. Once it has gone nothing can be done about it. Despondency can be transmitted to the rest of the side and your 'keeping could be below par for the rest of the innings. So if you make an error, pick the ball up quickly and return it to the bowler or close fielder as though nothing had happened.

It is the next ball that matters. If you are depressed about your miss you are likely to miss the next chance, and if you are feeling shattered about two missed chances, the odds lengthen on your catching the third. But always quietly apologize to the bowler and the captain when you have the opportunity.

Analysis

The right time to make a self-analysis on your day's work behind the stumps is when play has ended. You must make an honest assessment of the degree of difficulty of the chances that went

 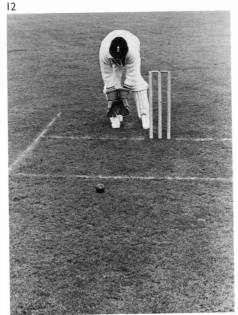 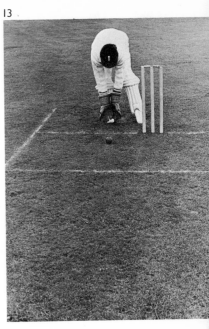

11. A good-length ball and the easiest to take. Knees are straight, hands move up as the ball comes off the ground and are directly behind the line with the eyes fixed on the ball.

12. This is a yorker to the batsman and the most difficult delivery to take. The head is lower because

the ball is pitching later. Because the ball is closer when it pitches the hands are not quite so high.

13. This is a yorker to the wicket-keeper. The hands are even closer to the ground because the ball has even less distance to travel to you after it pitches. Eyes should be firmly fixed on the ball.

astray and ask yourself, for example, whether you did not make the serious mistake of assuming that the batsman was going to hit the ball.

If the ball did not go cleanly into your hands you should analyse what part of the hands it hit and examine their position on trying to take the ball. Your coach can help you but it is important to make a close study of your own play so that in practice you can work hard to correct faults.

Practice

Practice is important. It is absolutely vital to have as much as you can, as often as you can.

When you have, say, a problem in taking a spinner, ask him to bowl at you for some time. At Test match practices on the Wednesdays, I often 'keep to the spinners in a vacant net asking

them to bowl at me individually and exactly as they would in a match, that is with the same run-up and at their normal pace. I encourage them to pitch quite a lot of balls well up to me, even with the occasional half-volley, so that I am accustomed to taking these rare and difficult deliveries (photos 11, 12 and 13).

Sometimes I put a stump in the ground to represent the bat. This can give the bowler a better idea of what length to bowl and also can give you deflections off the stump. A colleague batting can be a great help, especially if he plays with a stump or an old cut-down bat.

I am against going behind the stumps during net practice because a batsman usually has at least three bowlers and sometimes five or six different types bowling at him, giving a continual run of deliveries, so that the 'keeper is forever bending up and down. Having to retrieve many of the balls also makes it difficult for him to prepare for the next delivery. Thirdly, if the 'keeper wants to stand back there is rarely enough room for him to do so.

Training

During pre-season training a 'keeper's hands can come in for tremendous battering. If five players are in a squad throwing into the 'keeper he will have a day's returns concentrated into fifteen minutes with the ball coming to him at a considerable speed. So for training sessions I have a strong piece of sponge on top of my inners, covering just below the base of my fingers and the inside of the palm of my right hand. In two-handed catching my right hand is the more liable to bruising. The sponge is kept in place with a broad elasticated band which goes round the back of my hand. Derek Ufton, my ex-Kent colleague, not only gave me this tip but, on his retirement, his sponge protector which I still use today in practice.

I do a great deal of one-handed catching with somebody throwing the ball under-arm to either side of me. I do this first without diving. Then I place a stump either side of me at the full distance I can dive, always standing on a mark equi-distant between them (photos 14 and 15). A colleague, standing about ten to twelve feet away, flicks the ball quickly under-arm aiming for a spot just inside either stump (photo 15), preferably alternately to right and left.

If the 'keeper does not know which side the ball is going, it can be a very difficult exercise. The thrower should always make sure the 'keeper is back on his centre mark before throwing again. This practice is ideally done in front of netting or with two colleagues standing just behind the stumps so they can return any balls that happen to beat you!

On your own

If you have to practise alone, don't worry: there are ways and means of doing this and it is a fairly simple procedure.

The only ingredients required are a pair of pads, a tennis ball, a wall and a flat surface, such as a yard or garage drive. Stand twenty-five to thirty feet away from the wall and throw the ball against it so that on its return it pitches on a length in front of you, and you can take it as it rises from the ground.

Strap one pad round the other so that they stand up just in front of you and act as a wicket. Pads are preferable to stumps to avoid the risk of injuring the fingers by their continually striking wood while practising your stumping.

Using a tennis ball provides tremendous practice in taking cleanly, for unless you 'give' with the hands the ball will bounce out.

14

15

If you have a friend to practise with you, ask him to bat with a stump in front of the pads, but make sure that he holds the stump at the pointed end for safety. You can even chalk in a crease to add to the realism. The better the player, the more often he will hit the ball, but this is excellent training for a wicket-keeper, because when the striker does eventually miss or edge one you must still be ready for it.

Practice must be taken seriously. Make it as realistic as possible, and always do your utmost as you would in a match. If more than two of you are involved, then one of the others can stand behind you and throw the ball at the wall. This quickens your reactions even more because you cannot be sure of the ball's length or direction, when you are 'keeping, and throwing the ball yourself you naturally know roughly what length and direction the ball will rebound off the wall.

During pre-season training I go into the indoor nets for this drill because apart from being wonderful training it can provide great fun.

16. This was an outside edge by Imran Khan off the bowling of Bob Willis in the 1974 Oval Test against Pakistan. The ball went extremely quickly, a long way to my right. There was no slip and I really had to a make a tremendous amount of ground to make this catch right handed.

Equipment

The gloves

The most important part of a 'keeper's equipment is, of course, his wicket-keeping gloves, and here again, opinions vary as to the best type. Some like a supple pair with loose floppy fingers and hardly any front padding; others like heavy leather with plenty of protection. Mine come more in this second category than in the first.

Often a bystander has come up and queried their suppleness because he has seen me constantly closing my fingers into the palm, moulding the gloves into a cupping shape and making sure they never lose it. This shaping is something I do most of the time when I am not in action, such as when I am walking between wickets at the end of an over. Such exercise is not only good for the gloves but good for me in that it strengthens the fingers and hands, and so helps safeguard them against knocks.

My gloves are not as flexible as those of most other first-class 'keepers. The main reason is that I like strong leather on the backs. With a thinner type, I have always felt that my fingers push back easily, so I go for this extra support which helps a great deal to prevent this. What is more, such gloves will better keep the shape I have moulded them into.

When 'keepers rest their hands on the ground in the stance position, the leather wears away easily if it is thin. On the other hand, gloves of thicker material are obviously heavier.

The palms of my gloves are reasonably well padded to promote the feeling that the ball will sink into them rather than just strike my hands. But no 'keeper should have so much padding that it restricts the natural cupping and he cannot 'feel' the ball on catching it. The palms should be always pliable, and often the padding

17

on new gloves has to be softened by working in before use.

The gloves should follow the natural shape of your hands. If I place mine together ready to catch a ball, with the little finger of my right hand on top of that of my left, and turn the hands inwards slightly a cup is formed. The fingers should be relaxed and slightly curved forwards. They should also be comfortably spread apart, so forming a large landing area (figure 17). Strike a happy medium. Do not spread them so far that they become straight and stiff, or hold the fingers so close that the cup formed for catching is very small.

Catching cups and cupping your hands

With the method I have advocated, the hands form a large cup in which the ball can be caught safely most of the time! Nature provides a padding of muscle and flesh down the inside of each hand where they meet to form the centre of the cup. This is where we hope the main impact of the ball will be.

For me, the impact comes mainly on the flesh pads below the little and third fingers. The centre of the palms, which are naturally hollowed, give a large area into which the ball can fall, and act as the side walls of the cup (photo 18). If the centre of the palm was deeply padded then the cup formed would be much smaller. When the ball is caught properly, its full impact should rarely be felt at this point so that the part of the hands with the lightest protection should not be subjected to a continual hammering.

My reason for writing in some detail about the hands is that the gloves should follow their natural shape (photos 19 and 20), with the main padding down the inside of the palm and at the base of the fingers. The deepest and strongest padding in the best gloves comes therefore round the edge and at the tops of the palms; it becomes shallower towards the centre, where, in some, there is no padding at all apart from the leather cover.

It is also important to have the butt of the hand – the part just above the wrist – well protected because it is a sensitive area if the ball hits it with any force. For the same reason, I like normal, rather than short, cuffs which expose the wrists to injury from the ball which arrives almost on the half-volley and then bounces high.

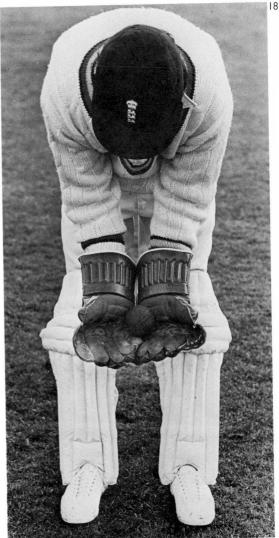

18. The two gloves have formed a large cup with its centre just below the base of the little fingers.

One-handed catching

I have explained one form of cupping the hands for catching, which is the usual method when taking the ball two-handed with the fingers pointing down or to one side. For one-handed catches, it is necessary to shape the hand so as to provide a different cup. Most 'keepers catch mainly with the index and second finger and thumb, with the ball centring just below the base of the first two (figure 21). I try for a position which centres the ball more under the index finger, making full use of the web stitched between it and the thumb. 'Keepers who prefer gloves without webs, seem to try and catch with the ball landing more under the base of the second finger.

The cup for the one-handed catch has three walls to it. The first wall is formed by the third and little finger being brought upwards so that

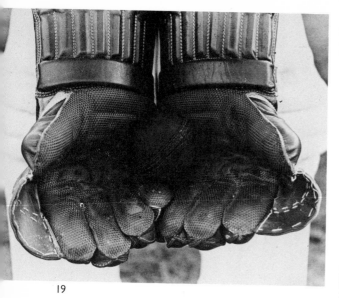

19

20

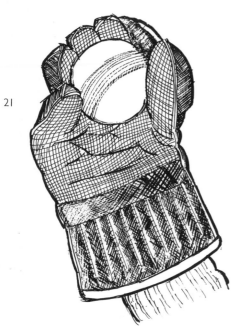

21

web is too loose it will not fulfil its role as part of the cup and the ball can easily squeeze out between the forefinger and thumb. If you misjudge the flight so that the ball strikes your

22

they face towards the thumb which, being raised slightly, becomes the second wall. The top of the web, from the tips of the forefinger to the thumb, then forms the third wall (photo 22). But the web should not be so taut that you lose the control and movement you need in the thumb; furthermore a ball striking an over-taut web will probably spring back out. Yet if the thumb, you may well need the support of a web to prevent the thumb being forced backwards.

The position of the thumb on the glove helps to make a large one-handed catching cup. You can judge for yourself by placing one of your hands palm upwards on a table with the thumb held out. You will then see that the thumb and the forefinger form a V width quite a distance between the top of the forefinger and where the thumb joins the palm. Yet on some gloves the thumb is set so high that this span is shorter than it should be and narrows your catching area accordingly. It is better and more comfortable to find a pair of gloves with the thumbs set low.

Catching overhead

For catching overhead another cupping shape is to be perfected. For this, I place the right forefinger and thumb on top, or in front of those of the left, the centre of the cup this time being where the two forefingers meet (photo 23). When I catch in this fashion, however, I tend to

23

take the ball mainly in my right hand, using the left as a side wall. Therefore I aim for the ball to land just below the base of the right forefinger.

Study the stitching lines on the palms of the gloves which break up the padding into different sections. These can be seen as outlines rather like a relief map under the outer rubber cover. One vital line runs along the bottom of each finger. This allows the fingers to move freely and naturally. In fact, nearly every line of stitching should represent a position which the hands will need to adopt. If it is difficult to cup your gloves, you might find that the palm has insufficient stitching or lines in the wrong place. Alternatively, the padding could be too firm and bulky.

Glove care

Most new gloves are a little stiff, especially in the palms. To loosen the padding and the stiffness from the glue binding the rubber surface, I put my gloves on the floor facing upwards and bang the palms with the toe-end of a bat. The next step is to put on the gloves without inners, and close my fingers over and over again, drawing the gloves into the various positions I need. I then do these cupping exercises with my inners on as well as my gloves. Now comes the time to use a ball, lobbing it from hand to hand and asking somebody to throw at me.

It is important to keep the various cupping shapes in mind, and refrain from twisting the gloves or pulling the fingers and thumbs backwards. If the glove fingers tend to fall back as you are about to take a catch there will be no support should the ball happen to strike on the top joints.

Badly shaped gloves might well force you into holding the gloves in the incorrect position which can make your hands and fingers tense. As with your inners, the gloves should fit comfortably without any feeling of restriction or fear that they are going to slip, even though only slightly. The finger-tips should be right to the end of the stalls.

Both gloves should be exactly alike. This may seem a strange thing to say, but sometimes a pair of gloves that are not similar at all slip out on to the market. By alike, I mean the padding should be similar, both in quantity and texture, and the outline of each glove should be identical from the cuff to the position and length of the thumb and length and thickness of the fingers. Unless each glove in a pair is made from the same leather, the feel between the two can be completely different.

Tape it

Sometimes a county 'keeper wears gloves with two fingers taped together. I have done this myself, taping the little finger of my left glove to the finger next to it after bruising its top joint while playing in the Pakistan Test at Edgbaston, in 1971 (photo 24). By taping a damaged finger to its next-door neighbour you add to its protection. If the ball strikes the damaged finger, the taping will prevent it being unduly forced back, but it must not cause any restriction.

24

Rubber facing

Make sure the rubber facing of your gloves is in good condition. Once it becomes smooth you are in trouble, especially when you have to take the field after rain. The wet ball and smooth surface will make catching as difficult as trying to grab a piece of soap in the bath water. So club

and school 'keepers should ensure that their gloves are resurfaced at the end of each season unless they have had little use. Mine are renovated in this way just over half-way through a season as well. As I am a county 'keeper, the manufacturers are helpful in rushing my gloves through, but such service would be impossible if every 'keeper wanted it at the same time, so make certain they are sent away during the winter.

If, unaccountably, you are caught with smooth rubber, here are two tips which might help. The first I have not used myself but it comes from Leslie Ames, the former Kent and England wicket-keeper, who told me he smeared eucalyptus oil on his gloves. This has the effect of slightly melting the rubber thus making it tacky. Obviously this must not be so overdone that it affects the ball. I can just imagine the expression on John Snow's face and his comments if, when he was bowling with a shiny new ball, I lobbed it back to him in a tacky condition.

My method, which I have had to use occasionally, is to drag a penknife across the rubber and use rough sandpaper on the smooth parts. This can only be regarded as a temporary expedient because when the treatment is repeated a couple of times pieces of rubber start to come away. So don't regard it as a long-term cure.

Hand care

Care of your hands is vital, of course. If they become bruised, the situation could arise that you do not want the ball to come to you, and that is a hopeless outlook.

Make sure your nails are not too long, to avoid the possibility of them buckling back or breaking completely. I tape any finger needing protection lightly with 'Prestoband' (photo 25), which looks like white gauze and does not stick to the skin but to itself. It needs a few attempts to achieve the knack of putting it on but, with a little practice, it can be applied easily. It is strong without being thick and bulky. I cut it into strips between four and five inches long and

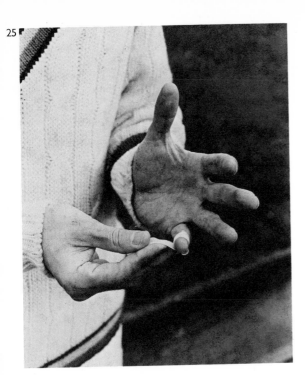

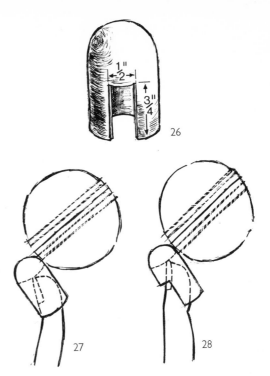

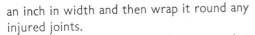

an inch in width and then wrap it round any injured joints.

Using a bulky tape, or putting too much tape on a damaged joint is a mistake, causing pressure if the finger only just squeezes into the glove.

Once in Australia, when I dived down the leg side, the ball struck the end joint of my right little finger. Bernard Thomas, the very sociable, versatile and pleasant Warwickshire physiotherapist, who was with us as assistant manager, came up with an ingenious suggestion.

His idea was to remove the little finger stall from the 'keeping glove and place it on top of my finger in exactly the same position that it would occupy inside. Bernard then cut out an area at the back of the stall about three-quarters of an inch long and half an inch wide. Stand the stall on a table and it looks like a little model igloo with a door (figure 26). It was the leverage of the top joint which caused me pain when this section was not cut away (figure 27).

With a section cut away there is nothing to force up against the back of the finger when the ball makes contact (figure 28).

If you ever have a damaged top joint and want to try this idea, make certain that the reshaped stall is glued back into the glove so that it cannot move from its correct position. If the cut out portion moves round to the front during play, then there is hardly any protection at all, and the original leverage problem still exists.

Inner secrets

The type of gloves to be used is a personal thing. Some 'keepers make do with little protection as they like to feel the ball as much as possible. Others wear a thin pair of cotton inners, yet with fairly well-padded 'keeping gloves. I must have fairly sensitive hands because I like well-padded gloves over two pairs of plain chamois leather inners, first a man's pair and then a large man's pair on top. These fit my hands comfortably, and while they are not tight enough to cause restriction they are not so loose that they drop away from my fingertips.

Between the two pairs of inners I place a strip of soft plasticine just below the base of the third

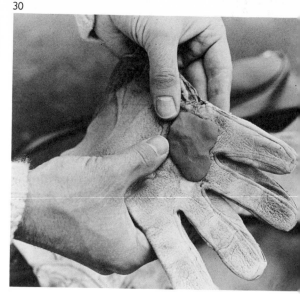

and little fingers, where I need the most protection (figures 29 and 30).

The plasticine should not be too thick, otherwise you will find that after the ball has pounded against it a few times it will spread uncomfortably over the palm of the hand. The best way to apply it is to put on the first pair of inners and then (photo 31), having moulded the plasticine into the desired shape, press it on top so that it sticks in place. When I slip on the larger inners I press them against the plasticine so that the whole becomes a unit. By pressing with the thumb of one hand through the top pair of inners of the other, it is easy to ensure that the plasticine is in the right place and kept pliable.

Leslie Ames, former Kent and England wicket-keeper, has told me that before the war he used a piece of steak against the palm of each hand on the inside of his inners. This not only gave protection but helped to draw out any bruising, but I know of no butcher these days prepared to supply me with steak for this purpose at anything like the low cost of my plasticine.

Inners made with a towelling wrist are handy. When there is a chance of a run-out by throwing the ball to either wicket a 'keeper needs to whip off a glove to achieve any force in his return. Inners without towelling will often

drag half off as well, rucking into a clumsy mess on your hand. This makes it impossible to throw accurately or with any power. But my inners do not have towelling wrists. Instead, I use sweatbands which can be pulled over so that they hold the inners neatly and comfortably.

Do I wet my inners? In county cricket I find this is unnecessary because, using them every day, they keep damp and pliable with the moisture from my hands. But when I played only once or twice a week, in school and club cricket, I found that between games the inners stiffened, especially if they were a little old.

So I always dampened them but refrained from soaking which makes the outside surfaces slippery, and tends to make the fingertips slide down against the rubber surface of the stalls. This has the effect of the gloves cupping slightly later than intended and means that your fingers are not right snug to the ends of the gloves.

The best way to dampen them is to wet the hand and flick the water on. This takes time to do properly, and I suppose the quickest method is to pass them under a fine shower, but such luxuries are rarely available. Submerging them in a basin of water involves heavy wringing out, risking damage and also the sliding sensation I have mentioned.

Leave your inners to dry naturally. Never put them in front of a fire or on a radiator as this

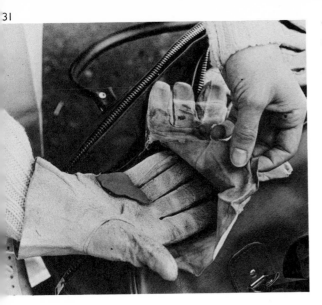

through the sole into the foot. When squatting behind the stumps, my weight is very much on the balls of my feet. Four to six hours of this, and I can start to feel every stud position. One remedy which I have tried is to have two pairs of boots with the studs in slightly different places. Then you can change them at the end of each session.

On hard grounds, I am tempted to wear crepe- or rubber-soled boots. The reason I rarely do so is that these increase the risk of slipping. Those troubled by studs hurting their feet, might find rubber inner soles a help, or alternatively, a very thin layer of steel sandwiched in the middle of the leather sole.

Studs

Studs should not be too long. A wicker-keeper must turn and twist quickly, often with all the weight on one foot. Long studs tend to become embedded deeply in the ground, thus holding the foot while the body is turning, which can give rise to ankle and knee injuries. Yet short studs obviously do not last as long, and unless they are changed as soon as they become ineffective you cannot move quickly and positively to the ball. So find a happy medium.

Like many county players, I take great care with my boots because you will realize how important it is to have them comfortable.

will soon make them brittle and they will eventually crack. Try to prevent them becoming hard and stiff, even out of season. With the necessity of caring for chamois, it is not surprising that many 'keepers favour cotton inners. Personally, I do not use them but they are preferred by some who do not like a great deal of protection on their hands.

Be happy with your kit

The most essential thing about your equipment generally is to be happy with it. I mean all your equipment, from your boots up to your cap. Occasionally, I have had to borrow kit, but this has invariably given me a feeling of uneasiness. The lesson is to try and keep to the equipment to which you are accustomed.

With cricket accessories the price they are today, few people can afford to buy a complete outfit for themselves but, when it is a case of using the contents from the school or club bag, always aim to pick out the same gear on each occasion so that you are familiar with it and more comfortable as a result.

Boots

Good boots are essential, and I look for those where the studs will not force their way up

Trousers

Some 'keepers like their trousers loose and baggy, so that they have complete freedom. Mine are long in the leg, mainly to stop them riding up over the bottom straps of my pads, but reasonably narrow and tight round the seat. A tight seat rather than a balloon effect gives some support to thighs and hamstrings when squatting, but it is necessary to ensure that the stitching is strong, particularly in the back seam! Fortunately my trousers have always stood the strain in first-class cricket, but twice, in youth representative games, they split. On one really hot day, I had to call for my only sweater, a long-sleeved one, to hide my embarrassment.

Protective measures

Protective measures are important. I like my shirts with sleeves long enough to ensure that when I have both arms extended I feel no pull on the wrists from the buttoned cuffs. There must be no restriction at all when stretching for those vital inches in taking a high return or wide catch. If your shirt sleeves are a little short and tight around the wrists ignore the buttons and use a small strip of plaster, preferably white. Place this on one side of the cuff, then pull the other cuff flap round to a comfortable position and stick the plaster down (photo 32). If it is necessary to leave a gap between the cuffs for stretching comfort, powder the plaster facing the skin. For a neater job the cuffs can be plastered from the inside of the shirt sleeve but this does not matter with wicket-keepers as the gloves will come over the top.

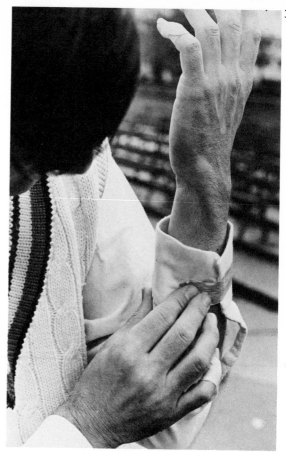

Sleeves down

When I was at school, and even during my first few county games, I conformed to the usual habit by having my sleeves rolled up. The result was that after several games I had to have treatment for grazed elbows, caused by grass burns when diving.

At Cardiff, in the next-to-last match of my first season in the Kent county side, former Glamorgan all-rounder, Peter Walker, edged one when I was standing up to Alan Dixon, that wonderful long-serving player.

The ball went in and out of my gloves and lobbed in the air. I dived forward on to the rock-hard wicket to take the catch and in the process tore the skin off both elbows. Two weeks after the end of the season, both arms turned septic, so I had to have them strapped in slings across my chest.

It so happened that about that time, Alan Brown, my former pace-bowling colleague, and myself were due for interviews for employment in the cement industry. Our prospective employers kindly talked to us over lunch at which Alan spent most of his time feeding me, as I could not lift my knife and fork.

Guarding against such injuries as far as possible seems to me a sensible precaution, and since playing with my sleeves down (photo 33), I cannot recall an occasion when I have drawn blood through my elbows sliding across the ground.

I also like a reasonably stiff collar to my shirt so that I can always have it turned up (photo 33). On hot days, this serves to keep the sun off the back of my neck and on cool and windy ones it acts as a draught excluder.

33. Remember the points I've mentioned in this section. Going from the top – Shirt collar up; Sleeves down; Cuff plastered; Top pad strap; Four straps instead of three; Two bottom pad straps.

Back flannel

Another part of my equipment is a back flannel. If you are doing your job properly you will be sweating from a very early stage in the game and when there is a stiff breeze blowing down the wicket your back will be exposed to it for half the time. Warm muscles with a layer of sweat on the skin could quickly stiffen in such circumstances.

Jack Jennings, the Northants' physiotherapist, who went to the West Indies with the MCC party in 1969–70, advised a back flannel, and how pleased I am I took his hint because back trouble can be an occupational hazard with wicket-keepers. Now I never field without one and I change it every session.

I always wear a vest too, but if you feel over-dressed then I would suggest dispensing with this and keeping the back flannel, which will always stay close to your skin. When I began in county cricket, I wore just a shirt but then, on advice, I added a vest and then the back flannel, and soon became used to wearing all three. They have certainly never restricted me.

Cap

A cap is not necessary for everybody although I always have one. It is obviously a help to protect your eyes from glare, especially for skied catches or from returns when facing the sun. With the longer hair styles in vogue today, caps have become more important for preventing hair obstructing the vision, and sometimes when the breeze has been strong enough for me to discard my cap I have sighed for the old short-back-and-sides days.

I was nearly put off wearing a cap by an extraordinary incident in a club match when I was fielding at first slip. The batsman went to cut and the ball flew to me like a rocket at chest height. I got my hands to the ball but fell back and could not hold it. As my head hit the ground, my cap was thrown forward over my face by the impact and the ball came to rest on my stomach. Not being able to see it and, wearing two sweaters, not being able to feel it

either I scrambled to my feet and the ball rolled to the ground so that the catch was not completed.

Pads

Now for some hints on your pads. People often ask if my pads are specially made. They are, and they are completely different from the ones I bat in. In fact they are only 24 in. high. For 'keeping, the pads need to be light and comfortable. Remember, they are a second line of defence, since the aim is always to play the ball with the hands. You should never be content just to pad away a throw-in that arrives short or on the half-volley. Yet some of the 'keeping pads on the market seem to be made with this padding away in view, big with floppy tops, flanges down each side and heavy bolsters.

I have never worn a pair like this, but they must be very tiring, as they tend to knock against each other, forcing the wearer to waddle like a man in a space suit. Apart from the restriction and discomfort, it is virtually impossible to sprint to the wicket in such cumbersome things.

Godfrey Evans has said that if people did not think he was showing off, he would have kept without pads. It is rare to see a county or Test 'keeper hit on the legs, which is just as well because the shins and knees are such sensitive areas which therefore need most protection. My pads have cloth-covered sponge strips, which are exceptionally light, running equally spaced out across the insides. The two for each shin are three inches wide and the one in the knee bolsters is an inch wide.

Straps

My top straps are sewn in about an inch above the three knee bolsters rather than on the middle one so preventing the top of the pads from flopping outwards. I found normal pads with the top strap on the knee a problem when I began in county cricket. If I misjudged the bounce and had to move my hands down to take the ball, my gloves were inclined to drop behind

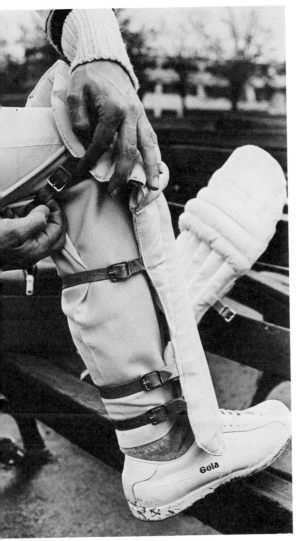

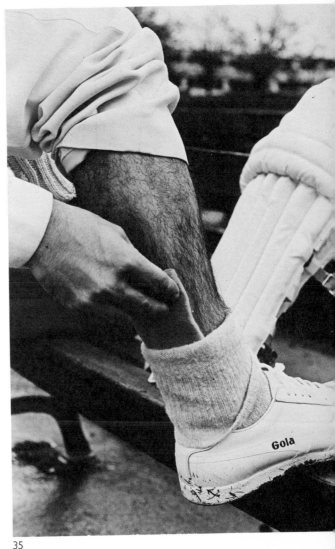

34

35

the top of the pads. With the knees even slightly bent, conventional straps will allow the pads to jut out away from the thighs, a handicap which can be avoided by moving the top strap higher as I have indicated. The tighter the top strap therefore the closer the pad will cling, but never buckle it so tightly that it affects bending and sprinting.

Some people tell me my pads look untidy and I must admit, having watched myself on television occasionally, that they don't look that neat. They swing to the side and the fact that I am slightly bow-legged does not help! The

reason is that I like the ankle straps buckled fairly loosely and the straps round my calves fixed so that I can hardly feel them against my legs. While I do not advocate that all other 'keepers should do this, I would hate to crouch all day with the straps tight.

In fact, I now have two straps at the bottom of each pad with a square piece of sponge inside the ankle of the sock against my Achilles tendon (photos 34 and 35). The combination of two straps and the sponge spreads the pressure over a greater area, and if the back of the ankle becomes stiff or sore, one strap can be released,

36

as its companion will still keep the pad in place. That is why I have four straps on each pad instead of the usual three (photo 36).

Abdominal protection

Some points I have mentioned may apply mainly to those 'keeping every day of the week, but I hope they prove of interest to players of all ages and standards.

Whatever the class of cricket, I think it is essential to wear a box (abdominal protection) which helps to instil confidence whether batting or wicket-keeping. On that subject my own view is that the strap-on box, with elasticated straps, is the best because it stays more easily in the correct position and doesn't ride up.

Methods and techniques

Preparing for the match

On match mornings I like to rise early to give myself ample time for preparation and the journey to the ground. My first aim is to do loosening and stretching exercises for between fifteen and thirty minutes. In Australia I recall how I used to creep out of my room at 7.30 to join our physio, Bernard Thomas, who is an ex-British international gymnast, and we would exercise together, as once this was done I felt ready for the day's work. As he roomed by himself there was no room-mate to disturb. If you care to follow suit I would advise you to consult a knowledgeable person first because exercises that are simple for one can be hard and dangerous for another.

I like to be on the cricket ground at least an hour before play. Once changed, I do a few more loosening and stretching exercises to offset possibly a long drive in the car. An hour's ride or more can stiffen the backs of the legs and, since the hamstrings and calf muscles are so important in our job, it is wise to look after them.

During some free winter months I had the good fortune to train with the Charlton Athletic soccer players. They were a wonderful team of people who taught me much about the right attitude and approach to professional sport. They always emphasized how important it was to loosen up before play or practice. How otherwise can you dive full length successfully to take a catch off the first ball of the day?

Loosening up

After a few exercises, I like to trot round the ground to prepare my legs for the running they will have to do in the field and the running I hope they will do if we are batting.

When it comes to practice, I have to do my share of bowling to the lads, and this gives me a chance to demonstrate my John Gleeson 'mystery' deliveries. The trouble is they don't baffle my colleagues to anything like the same extent as those from the Australian wizard himself did. I have mastered John's grip; the only trouble is I can't make the ball spin or pitch on a length!

If we are due to field, I return to the dressing room after my twenty- to thirty-minute loosener, just before the quarter-hour bell goes, so that I have plenty of time to prepare. I run a basin of water as hot as I can comfortably stand and submerge my hands until they are pleasantly warm. This was a tip I learned from the former Northants wicket-keeper and captain, Keith Andrew, who was one of the game's most helpful and friendly personalities.

I find, like everybody else, that I am keyed up just before taking the field. The effect of this often makes my hands go cold and holding them in hot water works wonders.

When there is no ready hot water, I put my hands together between my knees, rubbing them and pressing as hard as I can. Cold hands are a big handicap to a 'keeper. The fingers feel stiff, the ball stings and bruising is far more likely.

Nerves

Nerves, too, dry the mouth, and when the five-minute bell, or the 'worker' as it is known, goes, I pop in a piece of chewing gum. But I don't like constantly to run and jump with the gum in my mouth, and as soon as the dryness has gone, I remove it. The problem is then where to put it. Spectators have possibly seen me in an odd moment stalking about the end of the square like a gold prospector. The

37

38

probability is that I am seeking a suitable burial ground for the spent gum which sometimes finds its last resting place in an old stump hole!

Key man

Once the captain says, 'Right, lads, let's go,' a 'keeper should realize that he is a key man. His skill will give his bowlers confidence for he has far more chance in helping to dismiss a batsman than any other fielder. Keenness, vitality and general competence are the very cornerstone of the side's effort and his slick work can galvanize his colleagues even at the end of a long and tiring day.

Returns

Not the least important part of his work is in taking returns. Agility and anticipation can make even the bad throw look good. So don't just stand at the stumps and let a wild throw go flashing by. Move! Set everyone an example.

Be ready also to advise your skipper, if he approaches you on any situation or problem, for you are in a position to assess the strengths and weaknesses of a particular batsman and the nature of the wicket.

Stances

Just as a batsman has to have a stance so too does the wicket-keeper. Stances vary but one essential point to remember is comfort. It is no good copying someone else and then finding that their position imposes a strain.

Bending the knees fully helps to relax the back which otherwise might curve a great deal. The next thing to study is balance with the weight evenly distributed between your feet so that you are ready to move in any direction, but the most important factor is sighting the ball. In the stance position you should look at the ball with your eyes level (photo 37). To tilt the head on one side or turn it slightly means that you are trying to sight the ball unnaturally.

39   40

Another point is 'blinking'. Some people have higher 'blinking' rates than others, but when you are 'keeping you must make sure you never blink once the ball is on its way to you. In that fraction of a second that your eyes are closed, the ball might deviate and the necessary re-sighting could lose you the chance of a dismissal.

While waiting for the ball to be delivered some 'keepers place their hands on the ground between their legs. Others rest them on their knees (photo 38). In fact, most of the Australian 'keepers, including the great Wally Grout, have done this.

There are a few, too, who have their fingers resting on the ground outside their legs (photo 39). Jim Parks and the wonderfully energetic David Bairstow of Yorkshire use this type of stance. This is very comfortable, but I have found when standing up that sometimes I have been a little late in bringing my hands together. So if you use this stance make sure your hands are ready to work as a unit in taking.

Ex-Yorkshire wicket-keeper, Jimmy Binks, used to 'keep this way and he was one of the best I have seen standing up to the wicket. Once the ball was in his hands it was there to stay. I remember one incredible take by Jimmy when he was 'keeping for Yorkshire against Surrey in a Sunday League match. The last ball of the innings was to be bowled by England paceman, Chris Old, to Surrey wicket-keeper, Arnold 'Ob' Long. Jimmy decided to come up to the wicket for it and to everybody's surprise Chris bowled a bouncer. As 'Ob' Long ducked in disbelief, Jimmy not only took it with ease above his head but whipped off the bails and appealed for a stumping! The appeal was not upheld but if it had been it would have been one of the most remarkable stumpings I have seen.

Squatting

I like to squat with my hands placed on the ground between my legs, and when I am down I always keep on my toes (photo 40). This is not because it is necessarily the right thing to do, but because it is comfortable for me. When I have tried squatting with my heels on the ground I have to struggle to prevent myself from falling backwards. When I am squatting on my toes my weight is always slightly forward and I feel more ready to move off quickly.

Two of the many 'keepers who squat with their heels on the ground are Wasim Bari and Farokh Engineer, but when they take the ball the weight of their bodies is slightly forward on the balls of their feet, even though their heels are still in contact with the ground. This is important because they are then ready to move quickly and aggressively at the vital moment.

As the bowler comes in, I like to sway or rock gently from side to side, giving me the feeling that I am ready to move off in either direction, but I am very careful not to move my head.

Standing back

The first problem to settle when you are standing back is how far you go. Remember the aim should be to catch the ball just after it begins to drop in its trajectory towards you after pitching. Most 'keepers like to catch at about waist height when standing back, but I prefer to take the ball at knee height. This means I can stand an extra yard or so deeper and have that much more time to sight and move after the ball. This can be vital, especially when going for the wide deflections.

During the first few overs with the new ball the 'keeper has to judge the pace and bounce of the wicket, remembering also that the bowlers may be slightly below their full pace until they have completely loosened up. For the first over or so from each I stand a little closer than I would do normally because if an edge comes, it is better to be too near than too far away. True, the deflection can come to you very quickly and at an awkward height, but at least you have a chance which is denied to you if the ball bounces well before reaching your gloves.

Before the ball is bowled, I always scrape the ground with my studs to give me a standing mark (photo 41). This is just a guide which I can

41

change once the bowlers are delivering at their full pace.

Standing back in the stance position, I place myself wide of the off stump, so that I have a better chance of seeing a good-length ball *pitch* on the leg or middle stump. If you stand directly behind the line of the stumps you will not see those deliveries pitch because they will be hidden by the batsman's body or bat. To take up my position, move across so that when you are squatting you can see all three stumps at the other end and then go approximately twelve inches wider, so that you can see a gap between the two sets of stumps. As a general guide the nearer you are to the stumps when standing back (say to a medium-pacer) the smaller this gap will have to be. The closer you are to the batsman, the easier it is to see round his body.

The importance of seeing these good length deliveries pitching on leg or middle stump is that they might swing late or seam out towards the

42

43

off side. In both cases the ball could pass the off stump with you setting off down the leg side.

Some people feel that the difficult work is only done when standing up, and it has been said that when a 'keeper is standing back he is just a 'slip with gloves on'. This of course is terribly wrong. The ball even after pitching, can do all sorts of things. It can swing either way, dip or even rise on its way to your gloves. Those movements can be very late, and this means that you really have to watch the ball all the way into your gloves.

Colin Cowdrey, when fielding at first slip, said he studied the seam on the ball and this helped him to give his full concentration on it.

In England sides in which I have played, John Snow and Richard Hutton especially made the ball swing and dip late after pitching. Peter Lever deliveries, on the other hand, tended at times to rise suddenly as they approached you.

Sometimes the ball only swings after it pitches.

The absence of swing through the air is caused by the seam of the ball being slightly out of position as it leaves the bowler's hand but impact with the pitch adjusts it to the correct position with the result that the ball swings on its loop towards you.

The ball coming straight through can often bounce towards you at chest height. For a right-handed batsman, with the ball bouncing high and beating or getting a faint outside edge, I move to my left slightly inside the line of the ball turning my shoulders to the right taking it to the right of my chest (photo 42). If I move to my right and the edge is a little thicker than I judged, then I still have the problem of the chest-height catch with the ball following me.

Another way to take such awkward deliveries is to bend the knees slightly so that the ball comes at you neck or head level, catching it with the fingers pointing up (photo 43).

44. This time I'm on the wrong end of a diving catch. It's in the Third Test in Australia in 1974, at Melbourne, and I can only watch from the crease as Jeff Thomson's arms go up in delight as Rodney Marsh dives to take the catch which gives the Aussie paceman another Test wicket.

Diving catch

No greater thrill exists for me than to take off, stretching every inch of leg, body and arms to claw a wide deflection into my eager gloves.

Yes, I am talking first about the diving catch. For off-side edges that are thicker and so deviate away from you, you must move as quickly as you can and dive if necessary.

Strong and supple legs are needed to lift you from your squatting position to move before launching and making your attempt to catch.

It is rare in first-class cricket to see a 'keeper go for a two-handed diving catch in the same way as a goalkeeper goes down to save a shot. A goalkeeper can afford to ground the ball, but a wicket-keeper must keep the ball off the turf at all costs, so he forms his catching cup – the one we use most – with the little finger of each hand meeting.

A much wider span can be achieved by diving to take the ball one-handed. How great this difference is you can judge by standing against a wall with your hands and arms parallel to the ground in front of you. Now ask someone to act as a marker at the point where your fingertips reach and turn your body 90 degrees to the right or left with one shoulder still against the wall. Stretch out the arm which is not pressed against the wall and you will note that the fingertips are beyond your friend. In fact, the

45

Yorkshire Evening Post

distance gained when going for a one-handed catch is almost the width of your shoulders.

A 'keeper may think he can only reach the ball with one hand, and then, finding it not so wide as he first thought brings his other hand comfortably on top of the ball, as it enters the original glove.

For all diving catches it is necessary to avoid jarring the hands or forearms. So on taking the ball try and lift the gloves away from the ground, and land on the side of your body or even on your back.

Be natural

The essential point in taking diving catches is to be natural. Don't either stop your body from rolling over or exaggerate the roll so that you fail to concentrate on the ball. Wrestlers never stop themselves from rolling after they have been thrown, because they know that resistance to their fall could be dangerous. So let your body do the natural thing. Throw it and if you go with the ball and roll, you are much more likely to hold the catch.

I feel loosening exercises are a tremendous help to me in taking diving catches, especially the stretching ones for my shoulders, and arms.

Wasim and Farokh are both so flexible. They seem to stretch easily after the wide deflection. I have seen them take many wonderful diving catches, but Farokh is truly unbelievable. Apart from being supple, he is strongly built and his powerful legs take him over the ground quickly and give him a tremendous spring-off. I shall never forget Wasim's fantastic performance at Headingley where he did not take just one diving catch but five one-handers (photo 45).

He launched his slim wiry frame into mid-air to fasten on to every edge that came near him. His feat of equalling the world wicket-keeping record of eight catches in a match was richly deserved.

Sometimes a 'keeper will be criticized for diving when the deflection did not seem all that wide of him, but it all depends on the pace and the bounce. If the ball comes through normally, you may have a chance to move your feet and take the catch without diving, but sometimes it skids through quick and low, and you have no time to do more than dive after it.

Keeper or slip

In taking diving catches on the off side most 'keepers are set an unfair problem: you must only dive for those you feel will not carry to first slip. With such a thought in your mind it is likely that you will often fail to dive for edges which do not reach first slip. Once the stroke is made, you have a fraction of a second in which to make a decision. During any slight hesitation the chance will probably have gone.

I feel a 'keeper must be allowed to go freely for any catches he thinks he can take, so that there is no hesitation or half-hearted effort. When a 'keeper takes a one-handed catch in front of first slip's waist, it reveals that the fielder could be standing too close to him.

First slip should be one of the best catchers on the field and athletic enough to dive at full stretch. He should not stand so close to the 'keeper that he can only dive away from him. When an edge from a right-hander is going between the 'keeper and first slip, the 'keeper should dive to his right and slip to his left. First slip stands about two feet deeper so that on diving HIS hands come behind the 'keeper's hands forming a second line of defence – necessary because, standing where he does, slip has a fraction more time to sight the ball.

Only after some seven years in the game did I personally sort out this problem of diving for everything. During my Test career there have been two instances when I have started to go for a catch and then hesitated because the ball was going comfortably to first slip. The first was at the Oval against the Rest of the World, when Graeme Pollock edged Peter Lever. The ball was at chest height and I moved across and then stopped, thinking that the catch would be easier for Colin Cowdrey at slip. But my movement put him off and the chance went down. The other occasion was similar with Basil D'Oliveira at first slip. Again Peter Lever was the unlucky bowler as Doug Walters edged and my movement distracted d'Oliveira. After this last incident, first slip stood wider and I was given a free rein to go for everything.

The distance a 'keeper can cover depends on the bounce and speed of the delivery and where the ball finds the edge of the bat. If the ball is wide of the off stump and then deflected the 'keeper will have already moved across covering its trajectory. In these circumstances a 'keeper could take a catch in front of slip.

If, however, the ball is edged from off stump, the 'keeper, being behind the line of it, is that much further from first slip, so when he dives this time he will not reach in front of him.

Outside edge

The outside-edge catch which is most awkward to take is when the ball pitches on middle, or even leg stump with the batsman attempting to play to leg but the ball moves late, either in the air or off the pitch.

I have mentioned earlier that you should try to watch such deliveries pitch, but the difficulty comes when the bowler angles the delivery into the batsman's body and you set off to cover the line of the ball. For an outside edge in these circumstances you have both to refocus and change direction so that the gap between you and first slip has become quite wide. Such chances can prove elusive, though fortunately they are comparatively rare.

Inside edge

The most difficult catch to take standing back is the inside edge which usually occurs when the batsman intends to play a ball out on the off side.

Very rarely does an inside-edge chance come when a batsman has intended a shot to leg because part of his body is nearly always behind the line of the delivery.

Again the 'keeper, following the line of the ball, is looking for the outside edge when suddenly the ball comes through between the bat and the batsman's pads or body. Here again the 'keeper must make a quick change of direction but he will not be so tested often, because the ball often goes onto the batsman's pads or body, or even hits the stumps.

In Australia, I took what would have been my finest catch, during the last Test at Sydney. John Snow was bowling with the new ball to Keith Stackpole who managed a thick inside edge to a delivery about a foot outside his off stump. The ball flew wide to my left. I dived after it to hold the chance in my left hand. When I rose triumphant we found that the ball had just removed the off bail, so in fact, Keith was out bowled instead of caught.

All deliveries bowled down the leg side pass at some time out of the 'keeper's view but resighting is easier here because the ball generally continues on the line off which it rises from the pitch.

If the batsman gets an edge the ball will go still wider down the leg side and it is here that anticipation can be so vital. Always aim, therefore, to move beyond the original line of the ball as doing this puts you in position for a catch. If the batsman misses the ball and it comes through on its original line you should still be able to take it comfortably to the right of your body.

When Keith Andrew stood back he never squatted, but crouched like a goalkeeper with his knees relaxed and his trunk slightly forward. Keith used to make ground so quickly to wide deliveries and deflections, yet few realized he had moved.

I tried Keith's method for the first part of one season, but after a time my back ached so I went back to the squatting position but I would not turn you against Keith's method because it is very good and an easy one from which to move off.

Standing up

When Keith came up to the stumps he always went down and I cannot remember a class 'keeper who has not done so.

The reason is that most of your taking is low, especially on the Test wickets in England, and most of the wickets in Pakistan.

Only once have I experimented in not squatting when close to the stumps and that was on a wet 'turner' at Hastings with the ball bouncing high. Though the wicket was wet, the sun was out and at one end its rays were being reflected off a shining roof. While I was down I could hardly see the ball being bowled, yet the batsman seemed in no trouble since he was sighting the ball from higher up. With my head at a similar height to his I could see easily. This upright position worked well on that particular day, but then the majority of deliveries came through at above waist height, and I did not have to take one single ball at ankle height.

If you do not squat when standing up, you could find your view restricted by the batsman's body which would involve your taking up a position further outside the off stump to have a clear view of the ball. To stand wide is bad, since the bowler should be trying to hit the stumps, which means that your head should be as close to the off stump as possible to obtain a true line (photo 46). If you are positioned wide you could be taking basic deliveries, which are just missing the off stump, to the left-hand side of your body. When standing up, it is not necessary to place yourself wide to follow the good-length ball or half-volley pitching on the leg stump. You are now so close to the batsman you can see round him clearly and, in fact, watch off the pitch a good-length ball pitched just outside his legs. I think the closer you are to the stumps when standing up, the better (photo 46). You should be able to whip the bails off comfortably and not be so far away that you have to stretch or even take a short pace, which will cost valuable time when a stumping chance comes.

On the other hand you must not be so close that any movement on your part causes the bails to be dislodged. The distance back from the stumps varies, depending on the arm reach of the 'keeper. My toes are about sixteen inches from the return crease, but Godfrey Evans, for example, stood much further away than that.

As each delivery rises from the pitch, your hands should follow the bounce and direction of the ball. Coming up from the stance position, my heels go on the ground, although my weight is still mainly forward, so that I am now ready to move aggressively. Never be caught on your heels and leaning backwards.

Knees straight

Keeping your knees out of the way is another essential, which I achieve by taking the ball with my legs as straight as possible (photo 47). As the delivery comes through the air I start to straighten my legs from my stance position, always making sure that my hands are on the ground until the ball pitches. Don't put yourself in a position where your knees may restrict the movements of your hands.

Farokh provides an ideal model. From his

squatting stance he comes to a position where he is touching his toes with his fingers on the ground. As a result of this exercise his legs are loose and nearly always straight as he receives. If you take the ball, in front of your knees with the legs straight, your hands will have room to give back with the ball on the same line.

Methods of keeping the knees out of the way vary. Some 'keepers move one leg slightly backwards to create more giving room, but I feel this could possibly slow you down when you go for a stumping. Others spread their legs wide: the supple Wasim is one. Yet although his knees are always bent on taking the ball, they are so far apart that they never restrict him if he needs to move his hands slightly one way or the other to follow movement off the pitch or a deflection. If you cannot spread your knees as far apart as Wasim, be careful not to be caught in a position where your hands are trapped between your pads. As soon as you have taken and 'given' with the ball, you should be ready immediately to whip off the bails. To become a quick stumper, you must develop the habit of bringing your hands back towards the wicket after every ball, even if the batsman has played it. Don't take the bails off unnecessarily but always remove them if there is the slightest chance of the batsman being out of his ground. You can always help the umpire by mending the wicket once it is broken.

During the 1969 Test against New Zealand at the Oval, Bruce Taylor, attempting to sweep Derek Underwood, played over the top of the ball which came through to me. He did not appear to be stretched uncomfortably, but I went through the stumping motion and when I looked at the crease, Bruce's foot had dragged in front of the line and he was out. Had I not gone through the drill, the chance would have gone.

Behind the line

For deliveries coming through just outside the off stump, you should be directly behind the line of the ball. The wider the delivery, say to a right-hand batsman, the wider you will have to move your right foot across trying to make sure that you take it parallel with, or possibly forward but never backwards from, the return crease (photo 48). This movement brings your head on to, or as near the line of, the ball as possible. If the stride feels awkward you should allow your left foot to follow across naturally, so that you are again comfortable and balanced. But be careful not to move your left foot so far that you have difficulty in bringing your hands back to the wicket. I try never to take my left foot far away from the off stump, because the body weight would then no longer be 'attacking' the wicket, and I could not reach back comfortably. If the ball is that wide, I keep my head and body slightly inside the line.

Leg-side taking

For leg-side deliveries you must try and see the ball pitch before committing yourself to a movement. If you start off before seeing the ball pitch, you cannot know whether it will bounce high, keep low, or deviate. In fact, you will be gambling on where the ball is coming through.

When the ball is pitched right up just outside the batsman's legs, or even further than that, you cannot sight the ball off the pitch. But you will have logged in your mind the right line from its flight and moved your gloves behind it. You will then have to judge what height to hold your hands but with a ball of such full length the amount of lift should only be very small before reaching your gloves. Such deliveries can be extremely difficult to gather when they land in the rough caused by the bowler's footmarks.

Experience in 'keeping to the different bowlers in your side will be a great help. Study their pace off the wicket and the amount of bounce and movement they achieve off various types of surface. This will help develop your judgement, so that you are in the right position to take the ball cleanly.

When, standing up, I see the ball heading for the leg side I move my left foot slightly towards that side, remembering to keep my head as still as possible so that my eyes are peering round the batsman's body to watch the ball pitch. When I have moved my left foot across, my right

follows and then often I need to move my left again, so that I have covered a considerable amount of ground. But my body weight is still slightly towards the stumps (photo 49) and the cardinal point is to be able to bring the ball back to the wicket as quickly as possible. I try never to take my right foot so wide of the leg stump that my body is in a position where my hands cannot reach back to the bails (photo 50). To bring the ball back to the stumps with two hands means that for all wide deliveries you must turn your body, especially your shoulders, in to face the stumps so that both arms have the same reach towards the wicket (photo 51). Being right handed and catching with my little finger placed on top of the little finger of my left hand, I can easily transfer the ball into just my right hand. So when taking wide deliveries down the leg side to a right-hander, and down the off side to a left-hander, if I cannot comfortably reach the bails with both hands, I can in the same motion transfer the ball to my right glove, so that I have the extra reach needed.

One handed

This method of removing the bails with one hand is a a safety device if you happen to be too far away from the line of the stumps, but can also be used an an alternative method of stumping. Attempting a stumping with the ball in the right glove does not necessarily involve turning your shoulders inwards to face the wicket (photos 52 and 53). You can have them facing down the wicket or even turned slightly away from the stumps, and still reach the bails with your right hand.

Bob Taylor, the Derbyshire and England 'keeper, generally uses this one-handed method. He is an excellent all-round 'keeper, bubbling with energy and a great leg-side taker when standing up. I have seen him make some brilliant stumpings in this fashion, and one of them was in the State match at Perth during the 1970–1 Australian tour, when he stumped Derek Chadwick the Western Australian opening batsman, off the bowling of Geoff Boycott. It certainly gave great pleasure to the bowler!

Taking wide deliveries down the leg side to the left-hander or off side to a right-hander, I cannot go through the one-handed procedure. Transferring the ball to my right hand gains nothing and I find it very awkward and so time-wasting to transfer the ball from two hands into just my left. Left-handed 'keepers of course can use this one-handed method down the

opposite side from the right-hander. It is rather strange, but I can only remember seeing one left-handed wicket-keeper in first-class cricket and that is George Sharp, of Northamptonshire.

Standing up, it is generally harder to take deliveries when the batsman is playing forward, because the ball is pitched that much closer to you than when he is playing back. But a full half-volley is a simpler proposition than a ball pitching two to four feet in front of you. The half-volley can be taken just after it has hit the ground so there is no time for any unusual bounce or change of direction, but the ball pitching shorter, especially if it hits in the rough, has enough space to become unpredictable. The time left for you to detect any unusual movement is so brief that I feel these deliveries are the hardest to take cleanly.

A ball well up to the batsman outside his legs has a fair chance of coming through to the 'keeper. Most top-class players will try to sweep at these offerings from the spinners. The bowler doubtless did not intend to bowl it there anyway and a batsman, taken by surprise at its waywardness, will often be late with his shot. So for leg-side takes, the 'keeper has a natural sense of expectancy, far sharper than that for the ball

pitched well up on the off side, which will usually be hit comfortably.

The higher the class of cricket, the less likely the chance of a batsman missing these off-side deliveries. If he does, the ball usually passes under the bat or between bat and pad. On these rare occasions, the bat obstructs your view at some stage, and it requires non-stop concentration to be ready to make a clean take when this happens.

Stumping

Often people judge the difficulty of a stumping by the distance a batsman has advanced down the pitch (photo 55). This in most cases is a false assessment. When good players go down the wicket they always try to ensure that the ball does not beat the outside edge of the bat by moving themselves across covering its line. If a delivery does beat them in these circumstances, it means that they have again either played over the top or outside the line so that the ball squeezes through under the bat or between bat and pad. Again, the ball is hidden from the 'keeper at some stage. As the batsman is about to play his shot he might be only a foot out of his ground. He turns the delivery into a

54. A fine example of a one-handed stumping. Rodney Marsh is the 'keeper and John Snow is the unfortunate batsman. It just shows that the body does not have to be near the stumps.

55. This looks an easy one, but the ball had bounced and turned to give me what I consider to be one of my best stumpings ever.

56. I rated this my greatest catch when standing up. It was at the Oval in 1974 off the bowling of Derek Underwood. I had sighted the deflection from the batsman's forward defensive shot and dived full length to take a very difficult catch with my right hand.

yorker, but the momentum of his 'charge' takes him another two or three feet down the wicket by the time the ball arrives at the 'keeper. True, the 'keeper has the time to remove the bails but a successful stumping depends mainly on whether he resights the ball quickly enough to take it cleanly off this awkward full length.

If the batsman pushes forward and just drags his back foot as the ball beats the outside edge, the 'keeper can whip off the bails and be acclaimed for a wonderful stumping. But the truth is that the 'keeper has been able to follow the ball all the way and with more time to see it off the pitch, since it was not far enough up for the batsman to attempt anything else but a defensive shot.

The difficulty of a stumping chance should be judged mainly on these two points. Was the 'keeper unsighted at some stage? Where did the ball pitch? When a batsman plays forward defensively, the bat can be as much as eight feet in front of the 'keeper's eyes, which gives a stumper the chance to sight and move his gloves to follow a deflection. If, however, a batsman lays back, then his bat is very close to the 'keeper's gloves, and he will have no chance of seeing a deflection although, unless the edge is a thick one, the ball will not have space to deviate much from its original course.

Similarly with catches, many onlookers gain a false impression of the degree of difficulty, tending to base their opinion on how hard the batsman flashes at the ball. Remember, the

'keeper should always be watching the ball and not a violent movement of the bat. A faint edge will produce hardly any deviation, even from a batsman who is trying to hit the ball out of the ground.

Difficult chances

A way to evaluate the difficulty of a chance is to note where the ball goes after it has hit the 'keeper's gloves. If it drops towards slip, gully, leg-slip, or even goes square of the 'keeper, the edge was probably so thick that the ball hit the outside of one of his gloves, or possibly just a thumb. If for example the batsman achieves a thick bottom edge when cutting, the ball might only strike a 'keeper's fingers on the ends. Certainly these catches are the most difficult and many quite often hit part of the outside area of the catching cup formed with the gloves. But if the ball pops back out of the gloves and goes forward down the pitch, it can be assumed that it went cleanly into the cup and should have been held. Possibly the fault lay in failing to 'give' enough on taking it.

The really difficult catch standing up is again the inside edge, for you have only an instant to adjust your hands. But such chances are rare because, as we have said before, the ball

57

57. *Rodney Marsh caught off the bowling of Derek Underwood in the Fourth Test against Australia at Headingley in 1972. This was a thick edge down the leg side – always a difficult catch when standing up to the wicket. In fact this was a double deflection, from bat and body.*

generally goes on to the batsman's pad or body or hits the stumps.

Leg-side catch

Another rare catch when standing up is that on the leg side. Most top-class batsmen only drive through mid-on and mid-wicket, or glance when they have part of their pad or body behind the line of the ball so that any misjudgement on their part has much less chance of carrying to hand.

There is also the added difficulty of a double deflection from bat and body, which makes the catch extremely hard for a 'keeper standing up to take. But the most likely leg-side chance is when a spinner strays and the batsman sweeps too early or plays this shot too close to his body. In these circumstances, the ball can frequently strike the batsman on the gloves and pop up almost anywhere. I remember how in the 1968 Test series against Australia at Old Trafford John Edrich went to sweep off-spinner Bob Cowper. The ball ran off his gloves and lobbed over Barry Jarman's head, but he turned and dived away from the stumps to take a remarkable catch.

Up or back

One of the most important questions for wicket-keepers is when to stand up and when to stand back. Twenty years or more ago, 'keepers used to stand up to the medium and even medium-quick bowlers a great deal more than they do nowadays. Frankly, I think the change has been for the better because I cannot understand the point of all this standing up close to the wicket. Possibly, batsmen played forward far more than they do today, stretching uncomfortably to give stumping chances. Even so, looking back over the records there were not that many stumpings off medium-pacers.

In all the 51 Tests in which Alec Bedser played he took 236 wickets, and only three of those were stumpings. Alec Bedser liked his 'keeper close to the stumps because he felt it helped him in keeping on target. If bowlers feel that it helps them to bowl better, and results show this to be true, then the habit, of course, can be justified.

When I first played for Kent, Alan Dixon was usually one of the opening bowlers, and he liked the 'keeper standing up for his medium-paced swingers. Kent had had many years of 'keepers standing up to such bowlers and, being young and inexperienced, I followed tradition. For three seasons I stood up to Alan and in all that time I remember only three stumpings off him, and two of those could hardly be ranked as genuine.

The first was at Leicester when Peter Marner allowed a wide delivery to go down the leg side and, on watching me take the ball, unconsciously lifted his foot long enough for me to remove the bails. The other was at Canterbury against Somerset. Geoff 'Chimp' Clayton, that superbly safe ex-Somerset and Lancashire wicket-keeper, was batting with his ribs heavily strapped after injury. Alan again bowled a wide one down the leg side and Geoff, restricted and in pain as he was, practically fell out of his ground when he tried to follow the line of the ball.

As the years passed I came to realize that there was little point in standing up to Alan if there were no stumping chances coming, so back I went to a position where I could take the thick-edged catches I would have little or no chance of holding close to the stumps. Any catches, other than those edged fine, especially down the leg side, can be difficult standing up whereas standing back you will have far more chance of taking them comfortably.

A 'keeper should not stand up to a medium-paced or medium-quick bowler merely out of bravado. Nor should he do so just to save energy by not having to move and dive for the wide deflections, or sprint to the stumps to take returns. 'Keepers must be fit to do their job properly.

Another point to consider when deciding to stand up or not is whether you will manage to inhibit the batsman by doing so. County 'keepers, however, have to remember that some batsmen even deliberately stand out of their ground to the medium and medium-quick bowlers in an effort to entice the 'keeper up close. If they succeed, they then return to their crease, comforted by the knowledge that if they manage a thick edge the 'keeper is less likely to catch it and he might deflect catches to safety that first slip would have taken.

Batsmen who stand out of their ground are usually front-foot players, but, as they are that much closer, the ball comes on to them more quickly and the short delivery can have them in trouble. John Shepherd has taken many wickets by bowling bouncers at such batsmen, forcing them hurriedly to fend the ball away or go for the hook. But with the 'keeper standing up so that the batsman is confined to his crease, he has that extra yard or so in which to sight the short ball. So finally, a 'keeper must weigh up the possibilities of a stumping chance compared with the risk of missing catches. The key factor is to do what is best for the side and not just that which is showy.

If, however, you find in matches that you rarely stand up to medium-pacers, you should practise against their bowling close to the stumps, so that if the occasion arises when you are needed up at the wicket, you are ready to do the job capably.

Unusual chances

Many unusual chances come along, and a 'keeper must be prepared for anything. I remember at Cheltenham Alan Dixon was bowling

58

59

off-spinners on a turning wicket to Sid Russell, who edged one so that the ball became trapped between his thighs but did not lodge in his clothing. He did a hop or two down the pitch and I followed him so that when he parted his legs to let the ball drop to the ground, I was standing behind him, fell to my knees, put my hands between his ankles and took the catch.

Gordon Wilcox the young Worcestershire wicket-keeper achieved a remarkable dismissal when he caught Brian Close in a Sunday League game against Somerset. Brian top-edged a sweep and the ball flew high towards fine leg. Gordon turned, sprinted back and then dived to take the ball at full arms' stretch in front of him. When he landed, he was well over halfway to the boundary.

If the 'keeper feels he can catch a skier near the wicket and if his captain hasn't called, he must shout clearly 'mine' or ''keeper's catch' so that he can take it without fear of colliding with a colleague. The 'keeper should be the safest player on the field to take these catches.

Unusual stumping chances occur as well.

Whenever a batsman goes down the wicket and the ball hits his pad or body be prepared to sprint to the ball and return it to the wicket as quickly as possible. If the ball has rolled too far from the stumps for the 'keeper to bring it back in his hands he should flip it back. Flipping under-arm is quicker than a throw over a short distance.

I had rather an unusual stumping at Brisbane, where Ian Chappell charged Ray Illingworth. He drove the ball hard on to his ankle and it popped up in the air. I took the ball high in front of the stumps and whipped the bails off before Ian could regain his ground. Remember, the ball can be taken in front of the wicket when the batsman has played it.

I'll never forget Farokh Engineer catching John Edrich off the last ball of the fourth day in the first Test match against India at Lord's in 1971. John managed a thick edge off a ball from the left-arm spinner Bedi which, after hitting Farokh's gloves, fell almost to the ground when with his lightning reflexes he kicked it up and caught it.

Run-out

Run-out chances can also produce uncommon wicket-keeping techniques. For high returns I have cultivated a time-saving drill when forced to move back a pace or so, away from the stumps. I take the ball only in my right hand – and from above my head throw at the wicket (photos 58 and 59). To do this with certainty requires practice until you have absolute confidence in your one-hand taking and the accuracy of your throw.

Obviously it is safest when you are in a position where you can aim at all three stumps. Throwing when you are wearing a 'keeping glove can be very risky if you can only see one stump.

Talking of these run-out chances reminds me of when I was a victim myself. Kent were in Jersey playing representative sides out there as part of our pre-season training, and four Middlesex players guested for the Channel Islands. Among them was their England 'keeper, John Murray, who kept so consistently well at Lord's where the wicket often has an uneven bounce: it is not the easiest for the man behind the stumps, although it still remains my favourite English ground.

John, now retired, was standing up when I played a ball just behind square on the off side and set off for a single. In a flash he was on it, whipping off a glove and throwing in fast at the bowler's wicket. He achieved a direct hit while I was still at least a yard out of my ground.

John was a fine 'keeper, a very quick mover and adept at taking diving catches. In the Kent and Middlesex games in which I saw him he rarely made a mistake.

Fielding

As a schoolboy I hardly ever kept wicket and in club cricket never did. In fact I first joined the Kent staff not only as a wicket-keeper and batsman but also as an off-break bowler. In school and at club cricket I generally fielded first slip but this was not the case in the Kent second eleven where I had to do my duty in the covers.

If you saw me throw today it might surprise you to know that at the age of eleven I won a cricket ball throwing competition at my secondary school. But judo practice in the school playground resulted in a broken elbow and since then I've never had an Australian-type throw.

Having fielded in most positions in my early days has given me very valuable experience and helped me to understand the problem of the different fielders.

The performance of a wicket-keeper can be terribly important for the fielding side, especially in showing his enthusiasm for the game. If he's got energy and really enjoys his work, it can only serve to produce the same qualities in the rest of the field.

You will notice that most wicket-keepers when they move up to the stumps after the ball has been hit into the outfield, raise a hand to let the fielder concerned know exactly where to throw (photo 60).

This practice started, as far as I was concerned, when I first came into the Kent side. The other players suggested that because of my small size they couldn't see where I was too well. Raising my arm and hand in its red glove they said would give them something to pick out against

60

the white clothing of any other fielders close to the wicket.

Fielding is a very important part of the game and a vital catch or run-out can sometimes change the course of a match. I would advise all cricketers to enjoy their fielding and give it everything they've got. Not only will they find that their ability is improved but also it will prevent them from getting bored in the field. There's nothing worse for a fielding side than to find time begins to drag, for example in a Test match when you're struggling and basically just waiting for the opposition to declare. If you don't enjoy your fielding then your performance can really sag.

People of all generations argue whether the game has improved or not but I'm sure that even past players will never argue against the fact that

61. When you are taking a fielder's return get the stumps between yourself and the direction from which the ball is coming. Be close enough to the stumps to get those bails off as quickly as possible.

62

63

62. *Eyes on the ball, not on the target and moving at full speed. He is positioned so that the right foot will land as near to the ball as possible and could possibly act as a second line of defence if necessary.*

63. *Ball secure in hand, he looks up to assess the situation – will there be a run-out chance at one end?*

fielding today is of a higher standard than it's ever been. Certainly one-day cricket has helped in this respect for just one run in those competitions can be so vital. It means that no matter where you field you must dive after the ball to stop it if you possibly can.

Slip fielding

This can be a little like keeping wicket in that you must have tremendous patience and concentration. Like the wicket-keeper you must want catches to come your way and don't get impatient when they don't. You could spend a long day in the field and find that vital catch coming in the last half-hour, perhaps the only one you'll have had all day.

Like the wicket-keeper you must sight the

ball early and fielding at first slip to a bowler like Derek Underwood, for example, you must read the deliveries. Derek is famous for his very quick seamer and first slip must try and read when this is coming because he will need to move back a yard or so if he is going to take an edged ball from this particular delivery. If you stay in your original position, the ball will come far too quickly and you'll need a lot of luck to hold on to the catch.

On the other hand when the very slow delivery is bowled it's vital that the slip fielder comes closer, so that if the ball is edged it will carry to you. If you've stayed in your original position it will drop short. All this can only come with experience of the bowler concerned, and obviously at top level, where deliveries are disguised so well, it's difficult to know until his last stride. So first slip has really got to be concentrating and move quickly.

64

65

64. Left arm about to point towards target as right arm is cocked ready to explode into action, having spotted that the batsman will struggle to make his ground. Body weight is about to go on to right foot which, during the throwing action, will be transferred to the left foot, getting the body and weight into the throw. Aim about a foot to the left of the stumps to allow for body momentum taking the ball to the right.

I have always believed in a slip fielder slightly anticipating a catch which at times means moving slightly before the ball is edged. But great slip fielders like Peter Parfitt and Phil Sharpe will tell you they much prefer to stay still in case the ball doesn't go where you expect it. They feel that if you move, say to your right, and the batsman gets a very faint edge, the ball could go where you originally stood. It's very much a personal choice.

Covers

Cover has always been an extremely vital position although I do feel today that probably mid-wicket

65. A natural follow through is essential, head and eyes remain on target although throwing on the run.

is becoming just as important with the emphasis on players hitting a lot more on the onside than perhaps they used to a few years ago.

In the covers – and my remarks apply equally well to the mid-wicket position – it's important to be on the move when the batsman is playing his shot so that you are right on your toes to move off left or right to make a stop. Cover must be prepared to dive to stop the ball and he's obviously got to have a very strong and flat throw.

When he really becomes a top-class fielder in this position he's got to be able, having dived to stop the ball, to throw it in from the ground. Looking back to the time when South Africa were playing Test cricket, nobody will forget the brilliance in the covers of Colin Bland. He had all the assets I've mentioned as essential for a covers fielder.

I shall never forget watching him demonstrate

66. West Indies Captain Clive Lloyd demonstrates how his long strides and long reach benefit him when fielding in the covers.

before the television cameras at Canterbury his method of fielding practice. The ball would be hit to his left or right hand and he would run and throw to the stumps thirty yards away. Out of thirty throws I doubt whether he missed the stumps more than once. It just shows that practice can make perfect.

In today's game I should think that Clive Lloyd must rank number one in the covers. He's got the advantage of being so tall and agile. Although I'm only a small person I'm a great believer that the bigger they are the better they are. A person of Clive's height can cover so much more ground than the smaller man. He'll stop balls that other people probably couldn't get near.

England have no shortage of cover fielders and two newcomers to representative cricket, Graham Barlow of Middlesex and Derek Randall

67. *See what I mean about the swift reaction and movement of the bat and pad fielder. This picture shows Viswanath snapping up a catch off the bowling of Bedi to dismiss Lancashire's Harry Pilling playing for the MCC against the Indians at Lord's in 1974.*

of Nottinghamshire, have both shown what extremely fine fielders they are particularly in this position.

Bat and pad

This is a specialist position which has been spotlighted more since the change in the laws which limits the bowler to any two fielders behind the wicket on the leg side. Before the change you would see more leg slips, particularly to such bowlers as Alec Bedser, but afterwards it became the pattern to have only one leg slip with your second fielder on the fine leg boundary. This became your usual fielding pattern on the leg side behind the wicket, varied when the fielding side was on top by having both men close to the wicket. This means the introduction of the bat and pad fielder, in a short leg position just in front of square, close in on the leg side.

Fielders in this position try to get as close as possible and one of the best the game has seen was Surrey's Mickey Stewart, who used to take many catches for his county, a lot of them off the bowling of Alec Bedser, in a position which was vital to him when he bowled his inswingers. Although the position is vital to medium-paced and quick bowlers, it is probably seen to most advantage when off-spinners are operating on a turning wicket. The batsman is then confronted with the ball turning into him and quite often he will get an edge on to his pad or body and the ball will fly off to the waiting hands of the bat and pad fielder.

The greatest fielder I think I've seen in this specialized position is the Indian Test player Eknath Solkar; he plays most of his cricket on the turning wickets of his own country and has become a bat and pad expert, taking some truly miraculous catches. He has terrific speed of movement and even if the ball is edged in front of the wicket he seems to be able to spring off into a full-length dive, following the ball down the wicket, to take a brilliant catch. He also has

the courage – and that's a vital quality in this position – not to flinch. For if a batsman, instead of playing defensively, decides to attack, the ball could be travelling at up to 100 m.p.h. and if the close fielder is struck he could be very badly injured.

There are two reasons why your reflexes should be good when fielding in this position – first the need for quick movement to pick up a catch and secondly the speed of movement necessary to protect yourself if the batsman attacks.

The protective movement is to bring your hands, as placed in figure 68, straight up to cover your face as shown in figure 69. It's obvious then that the only place you can be hit is on the forearms. It takes a lot of courage but you must remember that the key word is PROTECTION not EVASION. I have seen more people hurt by trying to duck or weave out of the way. Surrey's Mike Edwards, under the tuition of Mickey Stewart, became one of the best bat and pad fielders in the country and his greatness lay in his marvellous ability to take up the ideal protective position. He received many hard blows on the forearms and shins but he never got badly hit on the head.

Bat and pad and indeed other close-to-the-

68

wicket positions have been criticized in recent years because of the obvious danger: the issue was spotlighted by the serious injury to Glamorgan's Roger Davis, who was saved by the kiss of life after being struck on the head.

Incidents of this kind generally lead to some debate on the question of wearing face masks. My own view is that fielders in this position should be allowed to wear face masks or some sort of headgear if they wish. I can't see any harm in playing safe. Batsmen I feel could be included too and I'll always remember when I was on tour with Kent in Canada a few years ago, how skipper Mike Denness went for treatment to a dentist, after receiving a blow in the mouth while batting. He was greeted with the remark from the dentist: 'Why weren't you wearing your face mask?' Whether the dentist had mistaken him for a basketball player or was being humorous I don't know, but was it such a funny remark to make? Why shouldn't cricketers wear some sort of facial protection?

Outfield

Fielding in the deep can be one of the most appealing aspects of the game. One of the first requirements of a good outfielder is to have a strong arm. You've got to be able to get distance and produce a flat trajectory so that the ball reaches the wicket-keeper just over the top of the stumps at terrific speed. It makes for the difference between a batsman being run out and gaining his ground fairly comfortably. Speed off the mark for the outfielders is essential – to put the batsman under pressure and perhaps to run him out. It will also help to take the catches because the quicker the fielder gets to the ball the better chance he's got of taking the catch. It makes life difficult for the batsman if he feels that he's got a good chance of being caught if he hits the ball in the air within thirty yards either side of a deep fielder.

I have been lucky enough to play in the same side as one of the finest outfielders the game has seen in Kent's Alan Ealham. His appearance is deceptive to batsmen until they know him because he is stockily built but he is one of the strongest and quickest movers I have seen. He has hands which live up to his nickame of 'Buckets' too.

The main thing about catches in the deep is to sight the ball early. Having done this try never to take your eyes off the ball even though you may be running. When it comes actually to taking the catch, remember two things. First, spread your hands out comfortably to form a large catching area and secondly, try and take the

71

ball at eye level or just below (see photo 70), bringing the ball down into your body after you have taken the catch.

If you think you may be fielding in the deep make sure you get some catching practice before the game starts. This will enable you to be accustomed to the different skies which you will play under from game to game. Unless it is really gloomy it is much easier to take a catch in the deep on a cloudy day than when the sky is bright and clear. Often the fielder's judgement can be impaired in bright conditions when it's

70. Notice the perfect hands position of Alan Ealham, my Kent colleague, as he prepares to take one of his many catches in the deep.

71. This is just one of those gully catches by Ashley Mallet. It was off the bowling of Jeff Thomson in the Second Test match between Australia and England at Perth in 1974, when the unlucky batsman was Geoff Arnold. No wonder the bowler and his fielding colleagues are applauding.

more difficult to judge how high the ball is and it appears to come down much quicker than you expect.

Gully

Generally there seem to be two types of gully position. If you're playing on a wicket which is helping the bowler, with the batsmen playing more defensively, you would stand quite close, looking for the ball to get an outside edge off the bat or for the ball that might pop up, perhaps hit the batsman's gloves, and resulting in the lobbed type of catch.

On good wickets, however, gully is generally deeper, looking to stop the cut or take a catch from a batsman playing the shot. It's vital from your gully position to study the batsman and particularly the bat. This will give you some indication of whether the ball may come your way, warning you to be prepared to make a diving stop or bring off what I call the Ashley Mallett type of catch. During the 1974–5 Test series in Australia, Mallett consistently took brilliant catches in the gully, mainly off the fast bowling of Dennis Lillee and Jeff Thomson, and frequently on his weaker side, diving to the left.

The attitude of mind you must develop when fielding in the gully is that no matter how hard the ball is hit you will always stop or catch it. Never be afraid that the ball will be travelling too quickly for you to handle.

Finally some basic tips to remember wherever you are fielding. It is important to watch your captain so that you can pick up any signal he makes for you to adjust your position. At times you can imagine you are the captain, because this will keep you interested and help your concentration which is so vital. Take any opportunity you can to get fielding practice, the more you have the better fielder you'll become.

Keeping fit

I firmly believe that any success I have had can be put down largely to physical fitness. Everyone should keep fit, that's my honest opinion. I regard it as my duty as a professional sportsman to be in top physical condition and I could find no excuse for me not being so.

For years you might have watched me performing all sorts of antics behind the stumps either between overs or at any spare moments during play.

Maybe they entertain the spectators, I hope so, but I can assure you that they are a serious and vital business for me. I know that some people get annoyed by them, some have written to me telling me so, but I regard them as an absolute necessity.

My colleagues in the Kent side pull my leg about some of the exercises. Frequently they have drawn laughter from the crowd by mimicking me.

All the exercises I do are important to me – for example, those involved with stretching the achilles, the calf muscles, the hamstrings and the back muscles. The object is to keep supple and be able to react instantly to a split-second situation. You can't move quickly if your body is cold and inactive. Diving catches and quick stumpings can be missed if you're stiffening up.

Keeping wicket calls for long periods of concentration. And to concentrate the mind must be fully active. I find keeping myself physically fit keeps me mentally alert.

I began to take physical fitness seriously when I had a serious injury playing for the MCC against Surrey at Lord's in 1963. I had a torn groin muscle and in the end finished up in hospital for a week. There I had the muscle stretched under anaesthetic.

Bill Tucker, the well-known London orthopaedic surgeon, explained how vital it was to keep loose and supple by stretching exercises and trying to avoid similar injuries in the future.

I had that week in hospital to digest everything he said. That was the beginning of my keep-fit campaign – and touch wood I've never missed any matches through a similar injury since.

Perhaps this will help explain just what I am doing and for what reason when you next see me behaving something like a cat on a hot tin roof behind the wicket. I'm convinced in my own mind it is this that has been such a great help in me reaching the top because naturally my muscles are stiff. Therefore, these exercises have helped me to keep them loose.

As I say, my exercises have provoked criticism but a lot of people over the years have written to me in a more enthusiastic way about them. I think for these interested people it's worth describing them in more detail.

First a preliminary word about warning your body and warming up. Before indulging in a sport which involves physical effort I like to warn my body of the stresses which lie ahead.

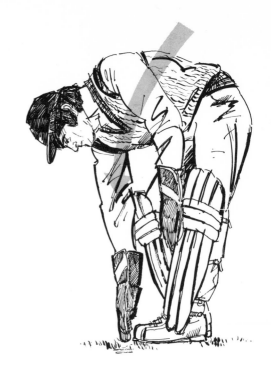

1: Toe touching

The best warning you can give is to ensure that the body is warm and that the muscles are supple and loose. So I suggest a simple exercise which can be done by anyone who wants to follow my warn and warm-up tip. With trunk forward and the back slightly bent, the arms are swung from side to side of the body. This is my first exercise of the day. It's simple and it's sensible. Try it sometime.

Relax the right knee and touch the toe of the left foot with the right hand so that it involves some body twist.

The exercise is basically to stretch the hamstring. On the low, slow wickets of England the ball generally comes through between the toes and the knees when I'm standing up to the stumps. I feel that it's vital for a 'keeper to be able to keep his hands close to the ground with his legs as straight as possible. You need to be supple and this is when the hamstrings are vital. This exercise helps me to get through my job and it's a precaution as well against injury.

2: Foot up

Bend the right leg upwards and behind, catch the foot in the right hand and draw it up against your bottom.

Basically this is a relaxing exercise – helping to relax the hamstrings and calf muscles after all the stretching involved in wicket-keeping in general and after the toe-touching exercise in particular. It also stretches the thigh muscles – an important aid for moving about quickly.

3: Knee squeeze

Bend the right knee upwards in front of you, clasp the leg with both hands round the shin and press the knee towards your chest.

This is an alternative relaxing exercise – for calf muscles and hamstrings after all the stretching you've done.

4: Groin stretch

With your legs a comfortable distance apart – for me that's about three feet – put your right hand on your right knee with left hand on left hip. The left hand is used to push the left leg down, stretching the inside of the leg.

The groins are very important when you move off to take the ball down the leg side, particularly standing up to the wicket. The more distance you can get, putting the leg across, the better it is. The exercise helps me to spread the legs and also helps to prevent troublesome groin injuries. Generally, keeping the groins supple helps you in running and sprinting and there's a lot of that for a 'keeper, especially when standing back.

5: Back exercise

The exercise involves a simple movement, basically it's a body rotation. You swing your arms from side to side, letting them take the body round.

This is designed to ensure mobility. It may make me look like a matador in a bullring – but it's important. Everyone needs a supple back, even office workers who might have to turn round suddenly to reach a file. It's vital for me so that I can turn from side to side to take a ball which may be passing wide of the wicket.

6: Leg-raise and rotate

Raise the knee to hip height or just above and rotate the knee outwards.

One of the most common injuries in sport and indeed in ordinary life is a strained groin muscle. Any sportsman will know that it can take a long time to get right. My leg-raising and rotating exercises are for groin stretching and hip mobility. It is an ungainly-looking exercise and one which seems to annoy some spectators. I'm sorry about that but it is as important to me as all the other exercises and I shall go on doing it.

7: A man and his horse

We have talked about how vital it is to have a supple back but another important point is that it needs to be kept very strong. It's been compared to a tree trunk controlling all branches of the human body. You can do this exercise lying face down on the floor. Lift your head and shoulders upwards. To begin with, try nine lifts in sets of three with a break of thirty seconds to a minute between each set of three lifts. Gradually build up the total of lifts as you get stronger. When your back gets stronger, if you visit a gym you can use a vaulting horse and a twelve-pound medicine ball. Lie across the horse, face downwards, with your trunk bent round it, arms hanging down one side and legs on the other. Put the medicine ball at the back of your neck, holding it with both hands and begin the lifts. Someone, preferably a qualified person, must hold you by the thighs while you raise your head up above the height of the horse.

8: Arm stretch

Lift each arm in turn, taking it backwards past your head. The movement is identical to that of a swimmer doing the backstroke. Stretch upwards as far as you can during this movement. This enables the muscles of the arm to be stretched and helps you to gain the vital inches you might need in diving for the ball. I find that the shoulders and arms must be loose and you must be able to stretch them to the full.

All these exercises should be repeated using the opposite limbs to those mentioned in the instructions given above.

Eating and drinking

Finally some hints which I follow as far as eating and drinking. I do both naturally. I take my food and drink the way nature intended them to be. I try to avoid any tinned foods which have been artificially coloured or preserved or to which anything artificial has been added.

I try not to take fizzy or artificially flavoured drinks. I do drink natural juices like orange, pineapple and lemon. As a sweetener in tea I prefer honey to sugar.

During main meals I try to avoid mixing proteins and starch. This means not mixing meat, especially red meat, with bread or potatoes. If I want potatoes I will have them with fish, eggs and cheese. I also like to take a little bit of salad with each meal.

During a meal I believe there should be a substantial break between a main course and a sweet. This is not always possible, but I try to allow for at least a short break.

I like fresh fruit and home-made pastry, providing it is made with whole wheat flour.

A good general tip is to leave the table feeling as though you could eat a little more. Don't leave the table feeling as though you couldn't eat again for a week.